Bugling Elk and Sleeping Grizzlies

The Who, What, and When of Yellowstone and Grand Teton National Parks

Shirley A. Craighead

FALCON®

GUILFORD, CONNECTICUT
HELENA, MONTANA

AN IMPRINT OF THE GLOBE PEQUOT PRESS

Falcon and FalconGuide are registered trademarks of The Globe Pequot Press.

Text design: Eileen Hine

Photo credits: pp. 1 (ravens), 2 (bald eagle, robin), 5 (mule deer), 7 (raven eggs), 11 (baby robin), 14 (young robin), and 19 (elk calf) by Jana C. Smith; pp. 8 (Uinta), 9 (kestrel), 34 (bear den), and 36 (fishing) in the Craighead Collection; pp. 19 (swan and cygnets), 20 (moose and calf), and 24 (baby sandhill crane) by Thomas D. Mangelsen Inc. and Images of Nature Stock Agency, www.imagesofnaturestock.com. All other photos are by Dr. Frank C. Craighead Jr.

Library of Congress Cataloging-in-Publication Data

Craighead, Shirley A.
    Bugling elk & sleeping grizzlies : the who, what, and when of the Yellowstone ecosystem / Shirley A. Craighead. — 1st ed.
        p. cm.
    ISBN 0-7627-2864-7
    1. Ecology—Yellowstone National Park Region—Juvenile literature. 2. Phenology—Yellowstone National Park Region—Juvenile literature. I. Title: Bugling elk and sleeping grizzlies. II. Title.

QH105.W8C736 2004
508.787'52—dc22   2003057113

Printed in China
First Edition/First Printing

CAUTION: For the safety of visitors and wildlife, visitors to the park must remain at least 75 feet away from all wildlife and at least 300 feet away from bears. Visitors should never disturb young animals or nesting birds. Ingesting plant parts poses a potentially extreme health hazard and could result in sickness or even death. No one should attempt to use any wild plant for food or medicine without adequate training by a fully qualified professional. Children should always be accompanied by a knowledgeable adult when exploring the parks. All participants in the recreational activities suggested by this book must assume responsibility for their own actions and safety.

Foreword

One spring when I was visiting my brother Frank at his home in Moose, Wyoming, he pointed to the white flowers on the serviceberry bushes. "The sandhill crane eggs are hatching," he said, although he was at least a mile from their nesting sites. With that, the beaver meadows at the bottom of the Teton Mountains where the cranes nested became animated with life for me. I was fascinated. "What else does the serviceberry flower tell you?" I asked. "That the coyote pups are out of their dens," he answered, "and the harlequin ducks are back in the swift streams at the foot of those mountains." Frank went on, "And that the great horned owl fledglings are out of their nests and testing their hunting skills on the abundant and careless young deer mice." The blooming of one flower had connected Frank with a theater of captivating dramas.

When I asked how he knew all this, he said, "For everything there is a season. The flowering of certain plants announces such things as what the goats in the mountains are doing or the eagles along the river. All living things have their timing with the climate and each other."

Frank's words reminded me of our childhood and a practical connection between plant and animal. Every spring our dad, F. C. Craighead Sr., an entomologist/naturalist, said, "It's time to go fishing," when he saw the bloom on the shadbush. The shad run up the eastern rivers to spawn precisely when the shadbush blooms. Dad was amused by the connection, but Frank was fascinated. To learn more about phenology, he kept little notebooks in which he jotted down the events of nature and the dates they occurred.

Toward the end of his life (2001), after a brilliant scientific career with our brother John, studying wildflowers, birds of prey, grizzly bears, ravens, and wild rivers and introducing radio-tracking to wildlife biologists, Frank worked on his dream book, *For Everything There Is a Season* (1994, Falcon Publishing). He was enthusiastically assisted by his second wife, Shirley Craighead, who in working with him, became a world-class phenologist in her own right.

So it was fitting that when Frank's editor at Falcon asked Lance, Charlie, and Jana, Frank's children, to edit their father's wonderful book for young people, they answered as one: "Shirley must do it. *For Everything There Is a Season* is her book, too."

Jean Craighead George
Newbery Medal Winner for *Julie of the Wolves*
Newbery Honor Book *My Side of the Mountain*

Introduction

When we study the things in nature that recur year after year, such as the migration of birds, the blooming of wildflowers, and the ripening of fruit, this is called phenology. In this book you will find phenological observations made by Dr. Frank C. Craighead Jr. He lived in the Grand Teton–Yellowstone ecosystem, and he kept track of these observations for more than forty years. For example, when we see the first blossoms on the arrowleaf balsamroot, we know that the cow moose are giving birth to calves, and when the cottonwood fluff and seeds are filling the air, we know that the baby mountain bluebirds are leaving their nests.

This book will not necessarily help you to identify flowers, birds, or animals. You need a field guide for that. This book will help you study ecology, the relationship of animals and plants and their surroundings.

The shortest day of the year (December 21 or 22) has come and gone. Although daylight hours will get longer every day, the stormiest winter weather is still to come.

Even though it may appear that **everything is frozen,** active life goes on in the Yellowstone ecosystem. In the months of January and February, you may see a pair of **ravens** sitting side by side on a branch. They may be preening one another or playing together. They enjoy soaring along with the air currents—they might chase each other, entwining their claws, or even fly upside down.

One activity you won't observe is the birth of tiny grizzly bear cubs at the end of January or in early February. Each cub (usually two or three are born together) weighs about one and a half pounds and is covered with fine short hair. Mother grizzly and cubs remain in the den for at least another two months.

ravens

The **bald eagle,** our national bird, may start laying eggs around the end of February. At the same time Canada geese, often paired for life, return to claim old nest sites, which may be on islands in the Snake River. Occasionally the geese will have a nest in a tree.

Mountain bluebirds brighten the winter scene, the brilliant blue of the male easily recognized against a background of dazzling white snow. They are returning from the south. Some may stay in the area of Grand Teton and Yellowstone National Parks while others fly farther north before settling into a nesting territory.

In late February **robins** that have returned north early find food under spruce and fir trees where there are bare patches of ground. If the weather is warm and free of snowstorms, the robins stay. A sudden blizzard, however, will cause them to retreat south for a few more weeks.

The ground may look frozen and deserted, but the active birds will find the food necessary for survival. Bald eagles eat fish, Canada geese eat grasses and bugs, and bluebirds and robins prefer insects and worms.

bald eagle

robin

This early in the season, the arrival and activity of birds dominate the scene. Each year there may be as much as a month's difference in the return dates of birds from their winter territories. Pairs of **great horned owls** stay near each other—the male perching alone, the female on a nest in a nearby hollow tree. She may already be laying eggs or incubating. Great horned owls often stay year-round in the river bottoms and can be heard hooting day and night.

Animal tracks in the snow always give you a clue to the presence of mammals, even though the animals themselves may seldom be seen. The tracks of coyotes, badgers, porcupines, and many others are easy to find. Look closely, there may be a story written in the snow!

You may hear the calls of sandhill cranes returning from the south before you see them. You will be fortunate if you can see their unforgettable courtship dances. They hop and bow to each other while flapping their enormous wings.

badger tracks in the snow

great horned owl

3

In an early spring, snow begins to melt, and a spell of good weather will come to the valley. Some small **groups of elk** may start leaving the National Elk Refuge, their winter home. However, should a sudden snowstorm arrive, the elk will return to the refuge to await better weather for traveling north.

Porcupines remain in the forest all winter. They eat the soft inner bark of coniferous trees, so food is available even in the worst weather. The scars they leave on tree trunks and large limbs are easily spotted.

You can sign up for horse-drawn sleigh rides out onto the National Elk Refuge at the National Museum of Wildlife Art. Being out in the midst of an elk herd is an amazing experience.

Grand Teton National Park has guided snowshoe trips. They are great opportunities to go out with an expert and learn how to identify animal tracks, to listen for bird calls, and perhaps to spot some birds in the forest. Yellowstone National Park offers guided snow-shoe trips in Mammoth and West Yellowstone, but you need your own snowshoes. You may see snowshoe hare tracks. The hares themselves, however, are hard to see because of their white coats.

elk herd

porcupine

This is the time of the spring equinox. On about March 21 the days start to get longer than the nights. The word *equinox* also refers to September 23 (approximately), when the nights start to get longer than the days and the northern hemisphere begins its autumn season.

Look along the roadsides where the snow has melted, and you may see the blossoms of two of the earliest wildflowers. One is the tiny sagebrush buttercup whose shiny yellow petals are easy to spot. Often growing in the same area is the white and pink **spring beauty.**

midges in snow

Soil along streambeds has thawed. Robins and bluebirds, as well as geese, can now easily find worms and bugs. The **midges,** or snow mosquitoes, emerging from their snow tunnels will add variety to the diets of birds. Ski or snowshoe along the banks of the Snake River, and you should find midges where the snow meets the river.

Mule deer do not wander much in the winter. They save energy by congregating in areas protected from the harshest weather. If you see deer resting while you are out skiing, keep your distance. Deer lose valuable calories if they become frightened and run away.

spring beauty

mule deer

Red-tailed hawks may make their first appearance of the season, arriving from their wintering areas in Mexico and points farther south. They first show up south of Grand Teton National Park. Gradually the hawks will work their way north until they arrive at their former nest sites, which they have to defend against other raptors (birds of prey, such as bald eagles, great horned owls, and northern goshawks) who may want to take over the territory. One defense used by a red-tailed hawk is dive-bombing the intruder, dropping upon it with outspread talons.

Canada geese also defend their nest sites in the river bottom. They chase any intruders, wildly flapping their enormous wings. Geese have also been observed snapping their beaks at other geese entering their territory.

Now the mountain bluebird numbers increase, and they begin their search for suitable nesting territories. A well-placed birdhouse will invite them as will a hollow in an aspen tree or fence post.

Canada goose tracks

red-tailed hawk

Pick up current pamphlets on rules and regulations from Teton and Yellowstone park headquarters and watch for the opening day of cutthroat-trout fishing season (will be different for each park).

During the coldest winter weather, moose stay in willow stands that protect them against the wind and blowing snow. But as April begins, they gather on sagebrush flats to eat the tender new leaves of the bitterbrush. It's a golden opportunity for some good photographs, but remember that moose can be dangerous, so keep your distance (at least 75 feet away). Warning: An angry moose will rise up on its hind legs and crash down with its front hoofs onto a real or imagined danger. Don't you be the target of those deadly hoofs!

raven eggs

Look up "aspens" in a field guide so you will know how to recognize this tree. When you see its leaf buds noticeably enlarged, this will be a clue that some **ravens will be laying their greenish brown eggs.**

Some **Canada geese start their egg laying.** Most nests are on islands in the Snake River. The geese line their nests with down—the plumage under the feathers of the adult geese. When the goose leaves the nest, she will pull the down over the eggs to keep them warm.

Great horned owl eggs are hatching, and white-footed and deer mice are giving birth to young. This new supply of rodents helps adult owls secure food for their newborn owlets. It will also help parent coyotes feed their newborn pups.

Uinta ground squirrels awake from hibernation each year in early April. It doesn't matter if the ground is covered with two feet of snow: The predictable squirrels will appear on top of the white surface and become easy meals for the growing abundance of raptors.

Uinta ground squirrel

Canada goose eggs

Average number of eggs per species:

- Geese, 5
- Raven, 5
- Great horned owl, 2

Sage grouse are gathering on their strutting grounds, or leks—large, open grassy areas surrounded by sagebrush. The male grouse will inflate his neck sac and then deflate it with a loud popping sound. This is the grouse's mating ritual, performed in the presence of many females. **American kestrels,** the smallest falcons in the United States, arrive in search of their former nest sites. They may have to fight other species, especially starlings, to maintain ownership. Many songbirds are now appearing from the south. The western meadowlark is Wyoming's and Montana's state bird. The male sings from a conspicuous perch, such as a fence post or tall branch of sagebrush. Song sparrows, American goldfinches, and Cassin's finches have all returned from warmer southern climates.

American kestrel

Grizzlies have awoken from their winter sleep. If the snow is still deep and too soft for travel, they will stay close to their dens until conditions are better. Then they will search for food. When grizzlies hibernate, they eat no food, nor do they drink. This is possible because their kidneys differ from those of humans in that they recycle urine rather than excrete it. **Grizzlies can smell a decaying animal,** a choice food, from miles away. They are also alerted to food by ravens circling over a carcass, calling and yelling, awaiting the arrival of a bear that will open the tough skin so that all can eat.

a grizzly and some ravens feed on a carcass

9

yellowbells

There is a gradual increase in the kinds of wildflowers blooming. Most of these early bloomers are small, like **yellowbells** and the yellow violet. The developing leaves of death camas are poking above ground. The bulb of this plant is poisonous, so it is a good flower to recognize and avoid. Leaves of arrowleaf balsamroot are several inches high. Later its large yellow flowers will fill the landscape! Other flowers starting to bloom are shooting star, waterleaf, long-plumed avens, holly-grape, and Wyeth biscuitroot. Look them up in a field guide, so you will recognize them when you see them.

Red-tailed hawks are laying their eggs. Ravens are incubating, and bald eagles have hatched. Conspicuous yellow-headed blackbirds are returning at the same time **bison begin to give birth to their young.**

bison and young calves asleep in a field

baby robin

Snow should be almost gone. If spring weather arrives late, flower blossoms will also be delayed. The order of flowering is always the same, even though the blooming cycle may begin early or late due to weather.

As aspen leaves begin to unfold, the landscape takes on a yellow-green tinge. The developing leaves make it more difficult to locate **bird nests** and observe the activity surrounding them. (Watch all nests from a distance so adult birds behave normally. Otherwise they may flee, give alarm calls, or circle you.) The new greenery is a cue that ravens' eggs are hatching and red-tailed hawks are incubating. Mountain bluebirds and tree swallows are fighting over nest sites.

Horns	Antlers
Bony growths on the heads of certain hoofed mammals, such as bison. Horns are permanent.	Bony growths, which are usually branched, on the heads of some hoofed mammals. Antlers are shed each spring, and new, larger ones grow during the summer months.

pronghorn

The first **pronghorns** show up in the valley. They are arriving from their wintering groups about a hundred miles south of Jackson, Wyoming. People usually call these beautiful animals "antelope." They look and act like many kinds of African antelope, but they lack one major characteristic of true antelope—permanent, unbranched horns. The male does have a little "prong" that sticks out of his main horn, reflected in the common name of "pronghorn."

Canada goose goslings appear on streams, ponds, and rivers. They are able to swim a few hours after they hatch. Parent geese may lead these youngsters long distances to green meadows to eat tender shoots of grass. Other geese keep their young near the area of their birth, especially if there is sufficient food nearby.

Trumpeter swans are now nest building. They make large platforms out of stems, leaves, and roots of aquatic vegetation. You can often see them on Flat Creek at the north end of Jackson. You can also often see and hear noisy red-winged blackbirds as well as yellow-headed blackbirds in the swampy area surrounding Flat Creek.

High in the mountains, pikas (small mammals closely related to rabbits) are venturing out of the talus slides (huge rock piles) where they live year-round. If any grasses, wildflowers, or small herbs have appeared where snow has melted, the tiny pika will feed on them. Having exhausted the "haystacks" they made under the rocks last fall, pikas are ready for a new food supply. It will be a month or more until all the snow melts at their homes 6,000 to 7,000 feet above sea level.

By this time the **mountain bluebirds** and tree swallows have stopped squabbling over nest hollows, and the females are laying their eggs. Ravens are busily acquiring food for their nestlings. They forage in pairs and steal eggs from other birds. They also hunt mice and voles and scavenge in garbage.

mountain bluebird

Sagebrush buttercup and spring beauty may still be in bloom. They will be joined by **yellow-flowered groundsel** and early paintbrush. Warning: Visitors are not permitted to pick wildflowers in Yellowstone or Grand Teton. With a permit visitors may pick wildflowers in national forests.

Pronghorns will venture farther north in the park as the snow disappears. They are frequently seen on Antelope Flats near Moose, Wyoming, as well as on the west side of the Snake River in Grand Teton.

Mule deer, a forest animal, can be seen along woodland trails. The deer within Grand Teton or Yellowstone are not afraid of humans, so it is often easy to photograph them from a safe distance of 75 feet. It will be several weeks before fawns are born.

young robin

Early nesting robins may already have young. They can be seen busily searching grassy areas for worms. The western meadowlark, a ground nester, is incubating. The male will perch on a nearby fence post and sing a most melodious song.

Elk are still moving northward past Blacktail Butte in Grand Teton. Some will stay in the forests within the park, and some will go all the way up to Yellowstone. They will also be moving south from Montana, where the elevation is lower, into Yellowstone, where they will give birth to their young and spend the summer.

If there have been some good rains, **morels** appear. Search for these prized mushrooms beneath cottonwood trees in the river bottoms.

morel

elk tracks

14

Arrowleaf balsamroot and **Nelson's larkspur** are beginning to bloom. Mountain bluebell can be found nodding along trailsides. The hike up Snow King Mountain, just south of Jackson, showcases wildflowers now through late summer.

Kestrels are laying eggs. Their clutches may contain up to five eggs, and they need twenty-eight days of incubation. Great horned owls, now with young, can be heard hooting. Some tree swallows are already feeding their first of two broods. Different kinds of blackbirds (red-wings, yellow-headed, and cowbirds) are still flying in flocks.

Nelson's larkspur

Female grizzlies with cubs in tow are roaming the huge valleys in Yellowstone. The mothers teach the youngsters which vegetation they can eat. They will not hesitate to discipline (with a swat of a paw!) a cub that doesn't obey. A predator, such as a mountain lion, a wolf, or even an adult male bear, may kill an unruly cub that gets out of sight of its mother.

arrowleaf balsamroot

Many yellow flowers are in bloom at this time, including **arrowleaf balsamroot,** yellow violets, dandelions, and yellow-flowered groundsel. The white flowers of death camas are also in bloom. Be sure to notice this flower with the poisonous bulb.

You can start looking for the first **puffballs**. They may be as tiny as a quarter or bigger around than a child's head. Always review a field guide and check with a knowledgeable adult when trying to identify any type of mushroom.

Yellow-bellied marmots, northern flying squirrels, and muskrats are born late in May. These rodents have three to six babies at a time. The newborns often become food for young predators, such as mountain lions, coyotes, wolves, and pine martens.

children with puffballs

Beautiful little blue violets begin to show up as the yellow violets are dying.

Trumpeter swans are incubating eggs while sandhill crane babies, called colts, are hatching. Willow Flats, just north of Jackson Lake Dam, is a good place to spot sandhill crane families. In Yellowstone look in Hayden Valley and near Fountain Paint Pots, north of Old Faithful.

Coyote pups are out of the den. The parents are busy catching mice, voles, chipmunks, and Uinta ground squirrels to feed their hungry young. These are the same prey species that red-tailed hawks hunt.

At this time of year, the large male grizzlies and considerably smaller females, or sows, travel together. It is their mating season. Once mating is over, they do not stay together. The sows that have young just born the previous winter do not mate. A couple of sows with cubs may form a small group and stay together during the summer. A female bear will occasionally adopt the cubs of another sow.

coyote pup

Types of mice found in this area:

- Deer mouse
- Meadow mouse, or vole
- Western jumping mouse
- White-footed mouse
- Wood mouse

Predators and prey:

Birds of prey are birds—such as red-tailed hawks, owls, and Swainson's hawks—that eat small birds and mammals. Small birds and mammals eaten by birds of prey are known as prey species. Moose, deer, and other ungulates (hoofed mammals) are also considered prey species because predators—such as wolves and bears—eat them.

coyote track

17

Young great horned owls and ravens are fledging. Mountain bluebirds, robins, starlings, and red-tailed hawks are all busily feeding their babies.

The bright yellow flowers of hollygrape are blooming. Also look for the pink or **white flowers on huckleberry bushes**. They promise delicious fruit that ripens in August. Both of these plants bloom alongside forest trails.

Notice the white flowers of baneberries. These will develop into glossy red, pink, or white berries. Learn the characteristics of this plant, for these developing berries are poisonous and should never be eaten.

Cutthroat trout are spawning. In coarse gravel the female uses her tail to excavate a saucer-shaped depression called a redd. This is where she deposits her eggs. The male discharges milt to cover the eggs. Milt is a secretion of the male reproductive organs in fish. Many of the eggs deposited by the female will be eaten by whitefish.

huckleberry flowers

cutthroat trout

18

elk calf

trumpeter swan with cygnets

In the Lamar or Hayden Valleys of Yellowstone, watch for grizzlies. The spawning of cutthroat trout continues, and trout are a favorite grizzly bear food. Both grizzlies and wolves will prey upon newborn **elk calves** when they can find them. The cow elk keep their calves well hidden, usually in a forest glade. However, the calf in this photo is not hard to spot in this dandelion field in Grand Teton.

Trumpeter swans should be hatching. You may see the **cygnets** (baby swans) closely following their parents. Remember that Flat Creek at the north end of the town of Jackson is an excellent place to view waterbirds, but you must not disturb them by getting too close. Sandhill crane colts may also still be hatching.

Duration of incubation:

Hummingbirds, 14–16 days
Swans, 37 days
Usually the larger the bird, the longer the incubation.

19

Mid-June brings the summer solstice, the longest day of the year.
   Moose calves are taking their first tottering steps. Remember that while a cow moose is raising her young, she will not hesitate to attack. She can be as dangerous as a grizzly!

moose and calf

Pronghorn are giving birth. **Coyotes** and red foxes both have young to feed. They can be seen in open fields searching for meadow mice and ground squirrels.
   When you see death camas fading (remember that their bulb is poisonous), you'll know that the white-crowned sparrows are feeding their young. They are ground nesters often found under sagebrush bushes. Mountain bluebirds are leaving their nests for the season. The immature birds perch on telephone wires or in other open spots waiting for their parents to bring them a tasty insect.

coyote

young red-tailed hawks

Red-tailed hawks are already feed-ing their young. Red-tailed hawks are predators and would eat a meadowlark if they could catch it.

If you like to fish, you may be aware of the appearance of **salmon flies** along rivers. Baby kestrels are hatching at the same time.

Grizzlies are seeking the nutritious roots of some flowers. They will find these plant foods in the same places year after year. This ability to remember where they found food makes grizzlies dangerous to humans. If they find a bowl of dog food on your porch, you can be sure they will return to look for more!

All ungulates have now given birth. Bison calves are quite easy to spot. They are light brown in color and can be seen following their mothers throughout Yellowstone and on the sagebrush flats of Grand Teton. Elk calves and mule deer fawns still have their spots, so they can be difficult to see when lying in a shady area amid grasses and wildflowers. This protects them from their enemies.

salmon fly

21

In the **Yellowstone ecosystem** now, about 150 species of birds are busy with nesting activities. Birds are either building nests, laying eggs, incubating, feeding nestlings, or fledging their young.

Blue flax is at its most beautiful stage. These delicate flowers close at night and open in the morning, facing east as the sun rises high in the sky. By evening, having followed the sun all day, the flowers will be open facing west. Blue flax often grows along roadsides.

Cotton from the cottonwood trees floats through the air, the entwined seeds giving it enough weight to carry it to the ground. Though pretty, the cotton causes allergies in many people.

blue flax

Young bald eagles leave their nests; kestrels also fledge. The parent birds will keep feeding their young until they have learned to catch prey on their own. Young raptors can be hard to observe, so watch for the beautiful **blue and white columbine.** When it is at its peak of blooming, you will know that these young birds of prey are out of their nests.

The year's greatest variety of flower species are blooming now. Carry a field guide with you, and hike along the trails in either national park. See how many flowers you can identify.

The cutthroat spawning season ends in July.

columbine

Young sandhill cranes follow their parents through meadows or wetlands. If you see adult cranes feeding in a meadow, look carefully in the surrounding area. You may spot the rusty-brown young near their parents.

Harebells are at peak of blooming. This flower often lasts into the autumn. Dandelions also are still blooming when winter snows begin.

If you are hiking in the mountains, watch for the pika and listen for its calls. When danger is near, it makes a sharp bark to alert other pikas to take cover. At times you'll hear calls from several animals at once.

Some noxious weeds are in bloom now—Canada thistle, spotted knapweed, and leafy spurge.

baby sandhill crane

sandhill crane tracks

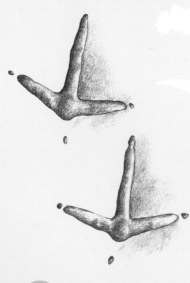

harebells

red buffalo berries

Many types of edible berries are beginning to ripen. Due to their appetizing appearance, **red buffalo berries** may fool you: They are not sweet! However, some Indians used them to make **"ice cream."** The Indians gathered the buffalo berries when they were at their ripest, added a sweetener and water, and then whipped them to a smooth froth.

girl eating "Indian ice cream"

coyote pup

Many young birds are fledging now. You will see immature white-crowned sparrows, yellow-headed blackbirds, and house wrens out of the nest but still being fed by a parent bird. Young ravens have replaced their down with shiny black feathers.

Gray wolves are now high in the hills surrounding the Lamar Valley of Yellowstone. They have followed the elk that climb to alpine meadows as soon as their calves are strong enough to travel. In Yellowstone elk are the most common prey of wolves.

Three-and-a-half-month-old **coyote pups** are learning to catch immature prey that have not yet learned how to protect themselves. The coyote pups themselves are preyed upon by wolves. The overall mortality (death rate) of young animals, both predators and prey, is high.

poisonous baneberries

Adult ravens are now getting new flight feathers, having recently molted. They need an abundance of food to complete this process, and they eat the young of many species of rodent as well as immature birds and grasshoppers. Some kestrels are still fledging, and they are vulnerable to predators for the first few days that they are out of the nest.

Thimbleberries, huckleberries, **holly-grapes,** and **poisonous baneberries** are all ripe.

Moose calves are a month old. Elk calves still have their spots. They lie down in a shady area, and while their mothers forage, they remain motionless to avoid detection by predators.

holly-grapes

Goldenrod and yellow sweet clover reach their peak of flowering. You will see the clover along roadsides in Grand Teton, especially along the road from Kelly up the Gros Ventre River. Yampa tubers, a favorite of **grizzlies,** are plentiful now. These tubers, which produce and store starch, taste like nuts.

By this time kestrels have all fledged and are flying well. Young ravens fly together in groups. If you see a raven landing awkwardly on a fence post, you will know you are watching a young bird. The parent ravens are still feeding them.

Corvidae

Family classification of birds that includes crows, ravens, and jays

sow grizzly and cubs

Huckleberries are ripe. They have such a strong aroma that you can often smell them while walking along the trails in the Tetons. Be wary of bears. They are as fond of huckleberries as we are and can frequently be seen greedily stuffing themselves. Bears are as likely to be close to a hiking path as they are to be in the backcountry.

Uinta ground squirrels are fat and ready to hibernate. Many have already gone underground. The last ones will disappear by mid-month and will not be seen until spring. These ground squirrels are true hibernators. When hibernating, their body temperature drops from 97 degrees to near freezing. They take only about four breaths a minute. These squirrels are so deeply asleep when hibernating, that if picked up, they would not awaken.

Young badgers and porcupines are four months old now. The badgers follow their parents through the sagebrush, intent on food and play. They eat mice, ground squirrels, and even insects. Immature porcupines—usually one per litter—spend their time in trees, eating the tender inner bark of trunks and limbs.

Uinta ground squirrels

young badger

badger tracks

29

Although many flowers have now gone to seed, there are still several species of flowers in bloom. But arrowleaf balsamroot and sticky geranium, so prominent a month ago, are brown and dry.

Thimbleberries, raspberries, and blue holly-grape are still ripening. Thimbleberry is in the same family as the raspberry. Thimbleberries are larger and much more delicate than raspberries, easily crushing as you pick them. The holly-grape, almost bitter when eaten along the trail, makes a delicious jelly when prepared alone or in combination with another fruit, such as **huckleberries.**

huckleberries

Flocks of birds increase in number. Immature mountain bluebirds and many species of swallows sit on power lines. You can easily count a hundred or more, all perched in a row.

Bison are starting their rut, or breeding season. In both Grand Teton and Yellowstone, you can drive alongside fields filled with bison during the rut. The huge bulls, huffing and grunting loudly, shove and battle each other for mates. Warning: Approaching bison at any time is very dangerous. Anyone attacked by a bison usually has to be hospitalized.

pine marten

Harebells and dandelions are still blooming. When you see these two flowers late in the fall, the flower heads will still be fresh and colorful.

A hard frost can come at this time of year and may result in the leaves of aspens and cottonwoods turning brown rather than shades of gold and yellow. In some cases the leaves may even fall while still green. The autumn season itself, recognized by its shorter days and lower temperatures, is caused by the tilt of the earth while it revolves around the sun.

Both the badger and the pine marten are breeding now. The **pine marten** is a mammal of the forest, spending its days and nights in treetops of lodgepole pine where one of its prey, the red squirrel, has its home.

Rabbitbrush, its yellow flowers very showy along the roadways, is at peak of blooming. This abundant plant causes serious allergic reactions in many people.

Pronghorns are gathering in groups prior to migration. Mice are storing seeds for winter. Red squirrels and least chipmunks are stockpiling unopened lodgepole pine cones, which will often be stolen by both black and grizzly bears. Least chipmunks are not true hibernators although some will fall into a rather deep sleep. They have good stockpiles of nuts and seeds beside them in their burrows. **Pikas,** those industrious little rabbitlike mammals living high in their mountain homes, are busy storing grasses and herbs under the rocks of talus slides. These will form their haystacks, which provide food for them during the entire winter.

pika

rabbitbrush

Mature bull elk may begin bugling, a vocal challenge to other bulls in the area. They are building up their harems, groups of cow elk, in preparation for the rut.

Mountain-ash berries are bright orange treats for bears. As you travel along a trail, you may come across bear scat, deeply colored and showing the half-digested berries.

As the temperature drops, grizzly bears start to prepare their **winter dens.** A grizzly usually digs its den at the base of a large tree on a north-facing slope. A black bear will use a natural cave. The black bear also will normally be asleep in its cave before the grizzly gives up and falls asleep for the winter. Both kinds of bears have about two more months to put on fat for their long winter sleep of five to six months. In contrast, Uinta ground squirrels hibernate for eight or nine months.

Some scattered flowers are still blooming, but the flower gardens are gone, replaced by dry leaves and stems.

Dr. Craighead studying a bear den

elk

As **the leaves are turning color,** the elk rut gets livelier. The males bugle more and use their huge antlers to fight any other bull elk entering their territory. Nightfall is often the best hour to hear and see the elk performing their ageless mating ritual. In Grand Teton ride along the park road on the west side of the Snake River to listen to the magical sound of **bull elk bugling.** In Yellowstone it is not unusual to see and hear the elk bugling outside Old Faithful Inn, in the Madison Junction area, or in Mammoth. Pronghorn males and bull moose may begin their rut now, too.

Canada geese can be seen flying south in formation. Many passerine birds, such as swallows, sparrows, and starlings, are now flocking. Bald eagles scavenge for food along the Snake River and other aquatic habitats.

Bull elk are still guarding their harems, so it isn't too late to venture into the park at dusk with the hope of hearing their bugles.

Fall **brown-trout fishing** may be starting, depending on the weather. The trout are beginning to move into spawning areas. The colder the temperature, the more apt the angler is to find browns ready to bite a streamer fly.

Most grizzlies are wandering around searching for scarce nuts, berries, green forage, and rodents. Bulbs of plants are also a good food source. The immature bears have to accumulate fat for their long winter sleep, and the mature bears, already fat, have to maintain their weight.

Dr. Craighead fishing Snake River

brown trout

The elk rut is just about over. Bugling is seldom heard. Most ungulates are now in some stage of their rut. Pronghorns are nearing the end of their mating season while mule deer mating is just beginning and will continue until December.

The sandhill cranes have left for their winter homes. Mountain bluebirds can still be seen flitting from fence post to fence post, often against a background of snow. Most songbirds that migrate have left the area.

Least chipmunks are still storing seeds for their winter food supply. They are often preyed upon by hungry migrating red-tailed hawks as well as by resident coyotes.

least chipmunk

chipmunk tracks

As snow storms pass through the northern Rockies, grizzly and black bears return to their previously prepared den sites. The bears may only rest outside and, if the weather improves, roam a little more until the next storm sends them back to their dens.

Bison in Grand Teton gradually head south to the National Elk Refuge. Swinging their massive heads back and forth, bison can clear away the snow and reach the dried grass underneath. Nonetheless, they seek lower ground where the snow is not so deep. They will spend the winter on the refuge. Some of Yellowstone's bison travel north into Montana where the elevation is lower and the snow not so deep. Others may stay around the thermal areas.

This is the hunting season. After killing an elk, a hunter guts it in the field, leaving the entrails for meat-eating animals to clean up. Many **bald eagles** arrive in the area and join the animals eating the guts. It's one of nature's mysteries how the eagles remember when and where to come for this food source. When the food dwindles, the eagles leave.

long-tailed weasel

The **long-tailed weasel** becomes an ermine now by shedding its brown fur and replacing it with a white coat. The tip of its tail is black. Sometimes you can spot a weasel that is in the process of turning white. It may still be half brown—quite conspicuous against a snowy background.

Elk now head south, some to the National Elk Refuge and others to smaller wintering areas. They usually move at night, but it is easy to see their tracks in the snow. Look along Highway 89 in the area of Moose village. In Yellowstone some elk migrate into Montana. Many stay around Mammoth, sleeping on the lawns of the park rangers' homes.

bald eagle

Pronghorn have left the Grand Teton area for the Red Desert of Wyoming, where snowfall is light. If they are caught by deep snow, they may not survive the long trek through the Gros Ventre watershed on their way there. Theirs is one of the longest migrations of mammals in North America.

Trumpeter swans can be found in several places with open water. Often there are thirty or forty birds on Flat Creek north of Jackson. These birds are very large, and they need a long water-runway when taking off. They sometimes become trapped in **ice** on little ponds or lakes when temperatures plunge rapidly, sometimes as much as 40 degrees from nightfall to dawn.

Grizzlies should now be sound asleep, snug in their beds of conifer boughs.

Plant-related phenological events stop now until warmer temperatures once again encourage new life. This is a dormant period for all plant life.

As you ski or snowshoe in different areas of the ecosystem, note the presence of animal tracks. If you note the tiny tracks of a **deer mouse** followed by those of a weasel, and then see the weasel's tracks continue without those of the deer mouse, you can imagine that the weasel enjoyed a tasty morsel.

Swans, geese, mallards, and other ducks still gather on the Snake River and open ponds. Moose are often found eating willows in protected areas of the river bottom.

deer mouse

41

bobcat

Nonhibernating predators and prey stay active despite the onset of winter. The predators include mountain lions, wolves, coyotes, lynx, **bobcats,** wolverines, weasels, martens, and badgers. The prey species include deer mice, meadow voles, pocket gophers, shrews, snowshoe hares, **red squirrels,** flying squirrels, deer, and elk.

You might enjoy a sleigh ride onto the National Elk Refuge. Dress warmly because this is the season of below zero temperatures and winds. Enjoy the wonderful photo opportunities.

red squirrel

Glossary

aquatic: found in the water or living in the water

brood: young hatched from eggs at one time

bugling: making a special mating call

bulb: usually an underground plant stem, having fleshy leaves like an onion

clutch: number of eggs being tended at one time

conifer: tree that bears cones

dormant: inactive; not actively growing

down: soft first plumage of many young birds; plumage under adult feathers

ecosystem: area shared by animals and plants interacting with each other and their environment

entrails: intestines or inner organs of an animal

ermine: term for a weasel that has acquired its white winter coat

falcon: bird of prey having long, pointed wings; very fast flyer

fledge: to grow the feathers necessary for flight

flock: to group together

forage: to search for food; edible plants

gills: organ by which a plant or fish obtains oxygen from the air

gone to seed: passing from the stage of blooming to the development of seed

gut: to remove the inner organs of an animal

harem: group of females

hibernate: to spend the winter in a deep sleep

immature: not yet adult

incubation: act of sitting on eggs in order to keep them warm until they hatch

lek: the strutting grounds of sage grouse and other bird and animal species

migrate: to move from one place to another

milt: secretion of the male reproductive organs in fish

mortality: being subject to death; death rate

northern hemisphere: northern half of the world

noxious weeds: introduced plants that take over both cultivated and uncultivated land

passerine: birds with feet that will grasp a perch such as a tree limb

plumage: feathers on a bird

preen: to clean, straighten feathers, or oil feathers

prey species: animals that are hunted by other animals for food

redd: saucer-shaped depression where a female fish deposits her eggs

rut: mating time for ungulates

scavenge: to feed on dead animals

spawn: to deposit eggs or sperm directly into the water, as fish do

spawning areas: gravel bars in streams, where water is rather shallow, yet has a moderate flow

talons: claws of a bird of prey

talus slides: piles of rock fragments at the bottom of cliffs

territory: a defended region or piece of land

thermal areas: places warmed by geysers, hot springs, or other types of steam vents found in Yellowstone

tuber: underground, fleshy thickening of the stem of many plants, such as potatoes

ungulate: hoofed mammal, such as moose, elk, deer, pronghorn, and bison

watershed: area that is drained by a river or stream

Bibliography

Craighead Jr., Frank C. *For Everything There Is a Season*. Helena, Mont.: Falcon Press, 1994.

———— *Track of the Grizzly*. San Francisco: Sierra Club Books, 1979.

Craighead, John J., and Frank C. Craighead Jr. *A Field Guide to Rocky Mountain Wildflowers*. Boston: Houghton Mifflin Company, 1963.

McEneaney, Terry. *Birds of Yellowstone*. Boulder, Colo.: Roberts Rinehart, Inc., 1988.

Minta, Kathryn A. *The Digging Badger*. New York: Dodd, Mead and Company, 1985.

Turbak, Gary. *Pronghorn: Portrait of the American Antelope*. Flagstaff, Ariz.: Northland Publishing, 1995.

About the Author

Shirley A. Craighead lives in Moose, Wyoming, in Grand Teton National Park. She worked closely with her late husband, Dr. Frank C. Craighead Jr., as he researched and wrote *For Everything There Is a Season*. She has hiked, fished, rafted, and observed flora and fauna throughout Grand Teton and Yellowstone National Parks for more than seventeen years. **Dr. Frank C. Craighead Jr.,** kept detailed, daily journals, recording the patterns of life that revolve around the changing seasons. He wrote *For Everything There Is a Season* (on which this book is based) after studying the plants and animals of the Yellowstone ecosystem for more than forty-five years.